HOMETOWN BANKING

A History of The First National Bank of El Dorado

El Dorado, Arkansas

Robert Dudley Sr.

Acknowledgement
The following made this book possible through their advice, providing data from internet surfing, written documents, typing manuscripts, offering encouragement and hope:
Steve Biernacki
Jeanie Bismark
Don Hale
George McWilliams
Shea Morgan
Owen Ostermueller
Darrin Riley
David Skinner

A special thanks to my wife Jane for her patience and support

Book design by Shea Morgan

Manufactured in the United States of America

ISBN 979-8-218-10048-3 (Paperback)
ISBN 979-8-218-10050-6 (eBook)

Library of Congress Control Number 2022920637

Historical references:

Dates and Data of Union County Arkansas 1541-1948
by Anna Harmon Cordell
Library of Congress Catalog Card Number 83-73730
Published 1984

Then and Now: A Guide to Historic Union County
by George Arnold and Shea Hutchens Wilson
Published 1994

Table of Contents

Foreward

In January of 1998 I retired from The First National Bank of El Dorado, Arkansas and its holding company First United Bancshares, Inc.

As a newcomer to both the city and the bank in 1962, I worked to learn about both. Harry W. Cawthon, Vice President and Cashier of the bank at the time, graciously shared many stories. When Mr. Cawthon retired, I occupied the position he had held. This included being Secretary of the Board of Directors and keeper of the records. While occupying this role, I was pleased to discover corporate documents dating back to the formation of the Bank. I share the contents of these documents and other information to give a perspective to The First National Bank and its place in El Dorado's history.

What follows is a result of gathering documents, conducting interviews, and seeking help from friends and family who generously gave of their time to navigate the internet for information. Throughout this process, my initial interest in the development of the bank has been overshadowed again and again by the rich stories of the people who shaped it.

In The Beginning

Union County was designated as such in 1829. Several years later, the city of El Dorado was legally incorporated in 1845. By the early 1890s, with the city's growing population and economic activity, businesspeople saw the need to establish a local bank.

On October 12, 1892, a Georgia native and local entrepreneur, B.W. Reeves, invited 25 businesspeople to his mercantile store to discuss the formation of a bank. One month later, the Bank of El Dorado was chartered as a state bank under Arkansas Law. B.W. Reeves was elected President, Jesse B. Moore as Vice President, and Sam Smith as Cashier. This bank failed before the national bank opened.

On May 9, 1902, the town's second bank, the Union County Bank in El Dorado, was incorporated with J.F. Sample as President.

In the summer of 1903, a charismatic entrepreneur with banking experience arrived in El Dorado with intent to enlist investors in the formation of a new local bank. Robert (a.k.a. R.D.) Duncan was employed as an assistant cashier of the First National Bank of Paragould, Arkansas. This bank was founded by the conversion of the Bank of Paragould, Arkansas from a State to a National Bank in June 1903. Duncan's work in El Dorado is evidenced by a document dated September 30, 1903. wThe letterhead of this document is the First National Bank of Paragould, Arkansas with the name R.D. Duncan as Assistant-Cashier and three other officers inscribed. This application document sets forth the terms and conditions for the creation and capitalization of The National Bank of El Dorado, Arkansas. Duncan and seventeen local people are listed as subscribers. Several names on the list stand out: Duncan becomes the largest shareholder with 120 shares; Mattie C. Wade, local businesswoman, is the second largest with 20 shares; followed by R.N. Garrett with 15; and B.W. Reeves with 10 shares. Of the names shown, two—Reeves and C.P. McHenry—had been associated with other local banks.

A document titled "Articles of Association" dated October 6, 1903, shows the directors as C.P. McHenry, B.W. Reeves, R.N. Garrett, M. Smith, W.M. Green and R.D. Duncan.

The Bank received its Charter Number 7046 issued to The National Bank of El Dorado. The first listed officers were B.W. Reeves as President, R.N. Garrett as First-Vice President, C.P. McHenry as Second-Vice President, and Albert Rowell as Cashier.

The bank opened its doors for business on the 9th day of December 1903.

A significant board meeting was held days later on December 14, 1903. First, the board elected Mrs. Mattie Carolyn Wade as a Director to replace W.M. Green. Second, a motion passed to convene a meeting of the stockholders on December 15, 1903 to vote on a proposal to change the name from The National Bank of El Dorado to The First National Bank of El Dorado.

The stockholders meeting was held as scheduled. A resolution to change the corporate name to The First National Bank of El Dorado was passed. The voting at the shareholders meeting revealed the following changes in ownership—B.W. Reeves now owned 30 shares, R.N. Garrett owned 25 shares, and M.C. Wade held 10 shares in her name and 20 shares in the capacity of a Guardian. R.D. Duncan kept 10 shares in his name and transferred 100 shares to a trust in the Fredericktown Trust Company of Fredericktown, Missouri. Also of note is that Duncan changed his address from Paragould, Arkansas to St. Louis, Missouri around this time.

TIMELINE

The First National Bank of El Dorado

SHARE EXCHANGE

Shareholders met and agreed to a share-for-share exchange with First United Bancshares, Inc. The plan was approved by regulators in 1981.

1981

2000

BANCORPSOUTH PURCHASE

First United Bancshares, Inc. sold all affiliate banks to BancorpSouth in September 2000. The First National Bank of El Dorado ceased to exist.

NEW CONSTRUCTION COMPLETE

Construction on the Garrett site was completed and the building was occupied by bank personnel in the Fall of 1974.

1974

1980

FIRST UNITED BANCSHARES, INC.

A new consolidation company, First United Bancshares, Inc., was formed by El Dorado executive leaders Gordon E. Parker, C.H. Murphy Jr. and H.C. McKinney, Jr.

DRIVE-THROUGH BANKING

Drive-through banking was introduced to El Dorado in 1960. The new facility used underground tubes to carry money and documents between the bank and drive-in.

1960

1968

GARRETT HOTEL SITE

The south half of the block was purchased in order to expand the bank property. This was the site of the Garrett Hotel. The hotel closed and the building was razed.

BANK OPENS

The National Bank of El Dorado opened its doors for business on December 9, 1903. Shortly thereafter, the name changed to The First National Bank of El Dorado.

1903

1921

EL DORADO'S OIL BOOM

On January 10, 1921, an oil well being drilled on the western edge of town blew in. Oil sprayed the area a mile around. El Dorado was overrun by people hoping to strike it rich.

A. BERTIG, PRESIDENT.
R. H. WEATHERLY, VICE-PREST.

6846.

J. H. KITCHENS, JR., CASHIER.
R. D. DUNCAN, ASST. CASHIER.

THE FIRST NATIONAL BANK
OF PARAGOULD.

CAPITAL $50,000.00. SURPLUS $5,000.00.

PARAGOULD, ARK.

We, the undersigned, hereby subscribe the number of shares set opposite our respective names, toward the Capital Stock of the proposed ~~[illegible]~~ National Bank of El Dorado Arkansas, now being organized. The Capital Stock of said bank is to be Twenty five thousand Dollars divided into two hundred & fifty shares of the par value of One hundred dollars each. One half of the amounts here subscribed is to be paid in on call of the president of said bank and the remainder in five equal monthly installments immediately following the completion of said organization.

El Dorado Ark. Sep 30th 1903

Names	Post Office		No. Shares	
C. P. McHenry	El Dorado	Ark.	10.	Shares
B W Reeder	do	do	10	" +
J M Smith	do		10	" ✓
W H Hutchinson	Do	Do	10	" ✓
W M Greer	Do	Do	10	" ✓
Mattie C. Wade	Do	Do	20	" ✓
W. R. Appleton	+ Do	Do	10	" ✓
Chas. L. Northam	Do.	Do.	[illegible]	" ✓
R K Garrett	"	"	15.	" ✓
R D Duncan	Paragould	Ark.	120	" ✓
W O Bryant	El Dorado	"	5.	" ✓
J R Mears	Do	"	2.	" ✓
A S Sorrells	Do	"	1	" ✓
W M Guilley	Do	"	1	" ✓
J S Cargile	"	"	15	" ✓
A T Goode	"	"	1	" ✓
J A S McWilliams	"	"	1	" ✓
J A Rowland	"	"	4	"
	Total		250	"

Thos Garrett [illegible] 916 Hammond Build.

Figure 1. Original charter application dated September 30, 1903. Written on The First National Bank of Paragould letterhead

TREASURY DEPARTMENT,
OFFICE OF COMPTROLLER OF THE CURRENCY.
Form 40.—Ed. 1 16 1903 2,000.

ORGANIZATION CERTIFICATE.

WE, the undersigned, whose names are specified in article fourth of this Certificate, having associated ourselves for the purpose of organizing an Association for carrying on the business of banking, under the laws of the United States, do make and execute the following Organization Certificate:

First. The title of the Association shall be *"The National Bank of El Dorado."*

Second. The said Association shall be located in the town *of* El Dorado*, County of* Union*, and State of* Arkansas*, where its operations of discount and deposit are to be carried on.*

Third The Capital Stock of this Association shall be Twenty five thousand *dollars ($*25000.00*), and the same shall be divided into* two hundred and fifty *shares of one hundred dollars each.*

Figure 2. Original Organization Certificate for *The National Bank of El Dorado.* Dated October 28, 1903

2

Fourth. The name and the residence of each Shareholder of this Association, with the number of shares held, are as follows:

	NAME.	RESIDENCE.		NO. OF SHARES.	
1	C. P. McHenry	El Dorado	Ark.	10	Shares
2	B. W. Reeves	Do	"	26	"
3	M. Smith	Do	"	10	"
4	W. H. Hutchinson	Do	"	10	"
5	W. M. Green	Do	"	10	"
6	Mattie C. Wade	Do	"	20	"
7	Chas L. Wortham	Do	"	5	"
8	R. N. Garrett	Do	"	30	"
9	R. D. Duncan	Paragould	"	120	"
10	W. P. Bryant	El Dorado	"	5	"
11	A. S. Sorrells	Do	"	1	"
12	W. M. Swilley	Do	"	1	"
13	A. N. Goode	Do	"	1	"
14	John A. McWilliams	Do	"	1	"
15					
16					
17					

3

Fifth. This Certificate is made in order that we may avail ourselves of the advantages of the aforesaid laws of the United States.

In witness whereof, we have hereunto set our hands, this 28th *day of* October, 1903

1 C. P. McHenry
2 B. W. Reeves
3 W. P. Bryant
4 R. N. Garrett
5 R. D. Duncan
6 A. N. Goode
7 A. S. Sorrells
8 W. M. Swilley
9 J. A. McWilliams
10 W. M. Green
11 W. H. Hutchinson
12 Mattie C. Wade,
13 Chas L. Wortham
14 [illegible]
15
16

Figure 3 and 4. Original Organization Certificate for *The National Bank of El Dorado.* Document notes shareholder names, number of shares held and witness signatures

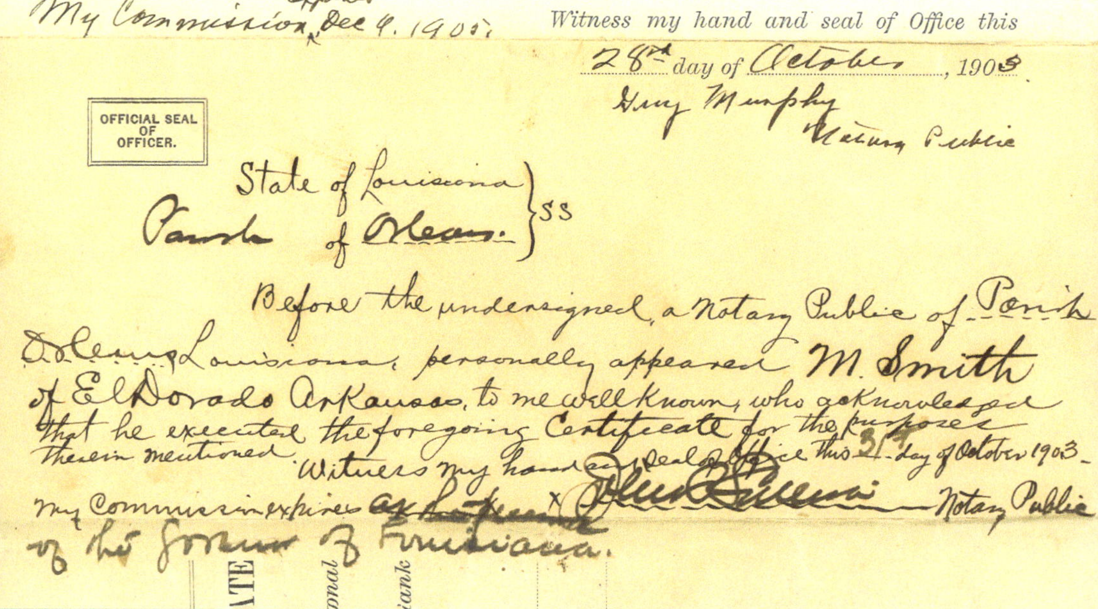

4

State of Arkansas
County of Union } *ss:*

Before the undersigned, a Notary Public *of* Union County, Arkansas

personally appeared

C. P. McHenry, B. W. Reeves, W. P. Bryant, R. N. Garrett, R. D. Duncan, A. V. Goode, A. A. Sorrells, W. M. [illegible], J. A. McWilliams, W. M. Green, W. H. Hutcheson, Mattie C. Wade and Chas. L. Wortham

to me well known, who severally acknowledged that they executed the foregoing Certificate for the purposes therein mentioned.

My Commission expires Dec 4. 1905. *Witness my hand and seal of Office this* 28th *day of* October, 1903.

Guy Murphy
Notary Public

OFFICIAL SEAL OF OFFICER.

State of Louisiana
Parish of Orleans } SS

Before the undersigned, a Notary Public of Parish Orleans Louisiana, personally appeared M. Smith of El Dorado Arkansas, to me well known, who acknowledged that he executed the foregoing Certificate for the purposes therein mentioned. Witness my hand and seal of office this 31 day of October 1903.

My Commission expires at [illegible] × [illegible] Notary Public of the [illegible] of Louisiana.

Figure 5. Notary registration of the Organization Certificate for *The National Bank of El Dorado*

CERTIFICATE FOR CERTIFIED COPY.

TREASURY DEPARTMENT,)
Office of the)ss:
Comptroller of the Currency.)

Under the provisions of Section 884 of the Revised Statutes of the United States, I, F. G. AWALT, Acting Comptroller of the Currency, do hereby certify that the paper hereto attached is a true and complete photostat copy of the original Articles of Association of "The National Bank of El Dorado" (Charter Number 7046), El Dorado, Arkansas,

and of the whole of such original on file and of record in this office.

IN TESTIMONY WHEREOF, I have hereunto subscribed my name and caused my seal of office to be affixed to these presents at the Treasury Department, in the City of Washington and District of Columbia, this 21st day of January, A. D. 1930.

F. G. Awalt

Acting Comptroller of the Currency.

Form 1980.
1-18-30---1000

Figure 6. Certification for the original Articles of Association for *The National Bank of El Dorado*

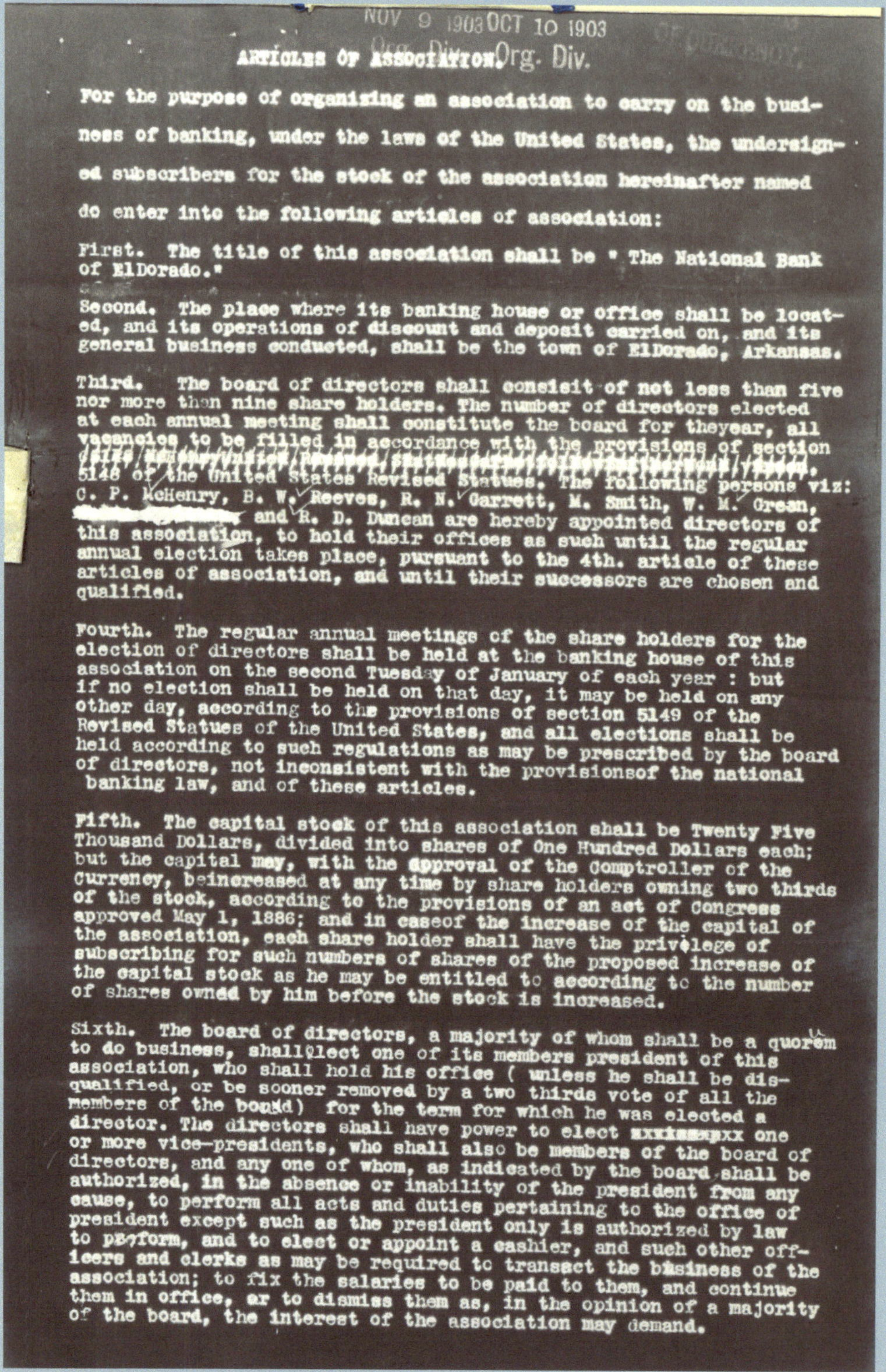

NOV 9 1903 OCT 10 1903
Org. Div. Org. Div.

ARTICLES OF ASSOCIATION.

For the purpose of organizing an association to carry on the business of banking, under the laws of the United States, the undersigned subscribers for the stock of the association hereinafter named do enter into the following articles of association:

First. The title of this association shall be " The National Bank of ElDorado."

Second. The place where its banking house or office shall be located, and its operations of discount and deposit carried on, and its general business conducted, shall be the town of ElDorado, Arkansas.

Third. The board of directors shall consisit of not less than five nor more than nine share holders. The number of directors elected at each annual meeting shall constitute the board for theyear, all vacancies to be filled in accordance with the provisions of section 5148 of the United States Revised Statues. The following persons viz: C. P. McHenry, B. W. Reeves, R. N. Garrett, M. Smith, W. M. Grean, and R. D. Duncan are hereby appointed directors of this association, to hold their offices as such until the regular annual election takes place, pursuant to the 4th. article of these articles of association, and until their successors are chosen and qualified.

Fourth. The regular annual meetings of the share holders for the election of directors shall be held at the banking house of this association on the second Tuesday of January of each year : but if no election shall be held on that day, it may be held on any other day, according to the provisions of section 5149 of the Revised Statues of the United States, and all elections shall be held according to such regulations as may be prescribed by the board of directors, not inconsistent with the provisionsof the national banking law, and of these articles.

Fifth. The capital stock of this association shall be Twenty Five Thousand Dollars, divided into shares of One Hundred Dollars each; but the capital may, with the approval of the Comptroller of the Currency, beincreased at any time by share holders owning two thirds of the stock, according to the provisions of an act of Congress approved May 1, 1886; and in caseof the increase of the capital of the association, each share holder shall have the privilege of subscribing for such numbers of shares of the proposed increase of the capital stock as he may be entitled to according to the number of shares owned by him before the stock is increased.

Sixth. The board of directors, a majority of whom shall be a quorum to do business, shall elect one of its members president of this association, who shall hold his office (unless he shall be disqualified, or be sooner removed by a two thirds vote of all the members of the board) for the term for which he was elected a director. The directors shall have power to elect one or more vice-presidents, who shall also be members of the board of directors, and any one of whom, as indicated by the board shall be authorized, in the absence or inability of the president from any cause, to perform all acts and duties pertaining to the office of president except such as the president only is authorized by law to perform, and to elect or appoint a cashier, and such other officers and clerks as may be required to transact the business of the association; to fix the salaries to be paid to them, and continue them in office, or to dismiss them as, in the opinion of a majority of the board, the interest of the association may demand.

Figure 7. Duplicate copy of the Articles of Association for *The National Bank of El Dorado*

The directors shall have power to define the duties of the officers and clerks of the association, to require bonds from them, andto fix the penalty thereof; to regulate the manner in which elections of directors shall be held, and to appoint judges of the elections; to make all bylaws that it may be proper for them to make not inconsistent with law, for the general regulation of the business of the association and the management of its affairs, and generally to do and to perform all acts that it may be legal for a board of directors to do and perform under the Revised Statues aforesaid.

Seventh. This association shall continue for a period of twenty years from the date of the execution of its organization certificate, unless sooner placed in voluntary liquidation by the act of its share holders owning at least two thirds of its stock, or other wise dissolved by authority of law.

Eight. These articles of association may be changed or amended at any time by share holders owning a majority of the stock of the association, in any manner not inconsisitent with law; and the board of directors, or any three share holdes , may call a meeting of the share holders for this or any other purpose, not inconsistent with law, by publishing notice thereof for thirty days in a newspaper published in the town, city, or county where the Bank is located, or by mailing to ech share holder notice in writing thirty days before the time fixed for the meeting .

In witness whereof we have hereunto set our hands this 6th day of October, 1903.

C. P. McKinney	El Dorado Ark	Subscriber for	10 Shares.
B. W. Reeves	El Dorado Ark	"	27
		"	
[illegible]	El Dorado Ark	"	10
[illegible]	El Dorado Ark	"	10
R. A. Duncon	[illegible] Ark	"	120
W. P. Bryant	El Dorado Ark	"	5
Mattie C. Wade	El Dorado Ark	"	20
W. H. Hutchinson	El Dorado Ark	"	10
[illegible]	El Dorado Ark	"	1
[illegible]	El Dorado Ark	"	1
[illegible]	El Dorado Ark	"	1
[illegible]	El Dorado Ark	"	5
R. N. Garrett	El Dorado Ark	"	30
		"	

I certify that these articles of association are executed in duplicate; that one of the instruments so executed is the foregoing; and that the other, alike in all respects is on file with said bank.

B. W. Reeves President.

Figure 8. Duplicate copy of the Articles of Association for *The National Bank of El Dorado, pg 2 and 3*

J. E. FRANKLIN, President.
G. W. LANPHER, Vice-Prest.

C. S. MARSH, Secretary.
J. F. GLAVES, Cashier.

FREDERICKTOWN TRUST COMPANY,

PAID UP CAPITAL $250,000.00
SURPLUS $31,250.00

Fredericktown, Mo., DEC 14 1902 190

Know all men by these presents, we The Fredericktown Trust Company do hereby appoint and constitute J. F. Tatum attorney and agent for us and in our name, place and stead to vote as our proxy at a meeting of the stockholders of the National Bank of ElDorado of ElDorado, Arkansas on Tuesday December the 15th. 1903 at three o'clock P.M. according to the number of shares standing in our name on the books of said bank.

FREDERICKTOWN TRUST COMPANY,
By C. S. Marsh Secretary.

J. E. FRANKLIN, President.
G. W. LANPHER, Vice-Prest.

C. S. MARSH, Secretary.
J. F. GLAVES, Cashier.

FREDERICKTOWN TRUST COMPANY,

PAID UP CAPITAL $250,000.00
SURPLUS $31,250.00

Fredericktown, Mo., DEC 15 1902 190

We hereby waive notice of a meeting of the stockholders of the National Bank of ElDorado to be held at their office in ElDorado, Arkansas on Tuesday December 15th. 1903 at three o'clock P.M.

Fredericktown Trust Co.
By C. S. Marsh secy.

Figure 9. Waiver of notice and proxy for board meeting of stockholders, dated December 1902

B. W. REEVES, President. | R. N. GARRETT, First Vice-President. | C. P. McHENRY, Second Vice-President. | ALBERT ROWELL, Cashier.

THE NATIONAL BANK OF EL DORADO.

EL DORADO, ARK., ________________ 190__

Special meeting of the Board of Directors of the National Bank of El Dorado, held at their office in El Dorado, Arkansas, on December, 14th, 1903, at ten o'clock A. M. Directors present: B. W. Reeves, C. P. McHenry, R. N. Garrett and R. D. Duncan.

On motion, Mrs M. C. Wade was elected director to fill the vacancy caused by Mr. W. M. Green selling his stock.

On motion, a meeting of the Stockholders of the Association was called for Tuesday, December, 15th, 1903, at 3 o'clock, P.M., to vote on the proposition of changing the name of the National Bank of El Dorado to " First National Bank of El Dorado."

On motion, the following resolution was adopted: Resolved that the Comptroller of Currency be, and he is hereby authorized to draw $6250.oo in United States Bonds, deposited with the Treasurer of the United States by this Babk to secure circulation, and described as follows:

$6250.oo of the loan of 1930 (2per cent), and that the Treasurer of the United States be, and he is hereby authorized to assign, and transfer the same to the Treasuere of the Unit d States in trust for the " First National Bank of El Dorado" to confirm to the change of title.

On motion adjourned.

B. W. Reeves,
President.

Attest:

Albert Rowell.

Figure 10. Board of Directors meeting on December 14, 1903

B. W. REEVES, PRESIDENT. | R. N. GARRETT, FIRST VICE-PRESIDENT. | C. P. McHENRY, SECOND VICE-PRESIDENT. | ALBERT ROWELL, CASHIER.

THE NATIONAL BANK OF EL DORADO.

EL DORADO, ARK., December, 15th 1903

Special meeting of the Stockholders of the National Bank of El Dorado, held this, the 15th day of December, 1903, at the office of said Bank in El Dorado, Arkansas. Mr. B. W. Reeves, President of the Bank, acted as Chairman of the meeting, and Albert Rowell acted as Secretary.

Secretary submitted waivers of notice of this meeting signed by all of the Stockholders of the Bank.

The following resolution was submitted and adopted by a vote of _______ shares, the same being more than two thirds of the total number of shares of stock of the organization; viz:

" RESOLVED, That under the provisions of the Act of May 1st, 1886, the corporated name of The National Bank of El Dorado is hereby changed to " The First National Bank of El Dorado."

The following Stockholders were present in person, or by proxy, and voted in favor of the resolution, viz:

B. W. Reeves,	El Dorado, Arkansas,	owner of	30	shares.
R. N. Garrett	" "	" "	25	"
C. P. McHenry	" "	" "	10	"
R. D. Duncan ,	St Louis, Mo.	" "	10	"
Albert Rowell,	El Dorado, Arkansas	" "	3	"
W. P. Bryant	" "	" "	10	"
R. B. Smith ,	Cargile, "	" "	2	"
J. O. Smith,	" "	" "	3	"
J. A. Rowland,	El Dorado, A "	" "	4	"
J. S. Cargile,	" "	" "	15	"
Mattie C. Wade,	" "	" "	10	"
M. C. Wade, Guardian,	" "	" "	20	"
Fredericktown Trust Co., Fredericktown, Mo., by ______________, proxy		" "	100	"

On motion adjourned.

Attest.

Secretary. Chairman .

Figure 11. Recorded minutes for stockholder meeting, dated December 15, 1903

B. W. REEVES, President. | R. N. GARRETT, First Vice-President. | C. P. McHENRY, Second Vice-President. | ALBERT ROWELL, Cashier.

THE NATIONAL BANK OF EL DORADO.

El Dorado, Ark., ______________ 190__

WAIVER OF NOTICE OF MEETING.

We, the undersigned stockholders of the National Bank of El Dorado, hereby waive notice of a meeting of the stockholders of said Bank to be held at the office of said Bank, in El Dorado, Arkansas, on Tuesday, December, 15th, 1903, at 3 o'clock P. M., to vote on the proposition to change the name of said Bank to " The First National Bank of El Dorado."

B W Reeves	W. M. Sevilley
R N Garrett	W. L. Rowell
C P McHenry	Mattie C. Wade
R L Duncan	M. C. Wade Gd
Albert Rowell	Mrs Bertha Davis
W. P. Bryant	J. A. McWilliams
J. B. Smith	
J. C. Smith	
J A Rowland	
J S Georgile	

Figure 12. Stockholder meeting, dated December 15, 1903. Attendees to vote on proposition to change the name to *The First National Bank of El Dorado*

Waiver of Notice of Meeting —

I hereby waive notice of a meeting of the shareholders of the National Bank of El Dorado, to be held at the office of said bank in El Dorado, Ark. on Tuesday Dec. 15th 1903. at 3 o'clock P.M.

[illegible]

New Orleans La,
Dec 14th 1903.

Waiver of Notice of Meeting.

I hereby waive notice of a meeting of the shareholders of the National Bank of El Dorado, to be held at the office of said bank in El Dorado Ark. on Tuesday Dec. 15th 1903 at 3 oclock P.M.

McMurrain Ark.
Dec 14, 1903.

Bertha Davis

Figure 13. Waiver of Notice of Meeting, dated December 14, 1903

District No. 8 *Charter No.* 7046 *No. of shares* 36

APPLICATION FOR STOCK

IN THE

FEDERAL RESERVE BANK OF ST. LOUIS

At a meeting of the Board of Directors of the First National Bank of El Dorado Ark, duly called and held on the 23rd day of April, 1914, the following resulution was offered, seconded and duly adopted:

WHEREAS, in accordance with Section 2 of the Act of Congress known as the Federal Reserve Act, approved on the 23d day of December, 1913, this bank duly notified the Reserve Bank Organization Committee of its intention to accept the provisions of the said Act and to subscribe to its proper proportion of the capital stock of the Federal Reserve Bank to be organized in this district;

AND WHEREAS, notice has been received from the Comptroller of the Currency that according to the certificate filed by said Organization Committee with the Comptroller designating the several Federal Reserve cities and defining the geographical limits of the districts to be respectively served by the Federal Reserve Banks located in such cities, this bank is located in District No. 8, which district will be served by the Federal Reserve Bank of St. Louis;

AND WHEREAS, six per cent of the unimpaired capital and surplus of this association amounts to Thirty six Hundred and no/100 Dollars;

NOW, THEREFORE, BE IT RESOLVED, that the president or vice-president and cashier of this bank be, and they are hereby authorized, empowered and directed to make application for and to subscribe to 36 shares, of a par value of $100 each, of the capital stock of the Federal Reserve Bank of St. Louis, now organizing, and to pay for such stock in accordance with the provisions of Section 2 of the said Federal Reserve Act as and when called upon by the Reserve Bank Organization Committee or by the Federal Reserve Board.

I hereby certify that the foregoing is a true and correct copy of a resolution passed by the Board of Directors of this association on the date specified.

Albert Stowell *Cashier,*

First *National Bank of* El Dorado Ark

Pursuant to the foregoing resolution the First N National Bank of El Dorado Ark hereby subscribes to and makes application for .... shares of the capital stock of the Federal Reserve Bank of St. Louis of a par value of $100 each, amounting to $................., and agrees to pay for same in accordance with the provisions of the Federal Reserve Act.

First NATIONAL BANK OF El Dorado Ark

(SEAL.) By R. N. Garrett *President.*

Attest: Albert Stowell *Cashier.*

To the RESERVE BANK ORGANIZATION COMMITTEE,
Washington, D. C.

Figure 14. Application for stock in the Federal Reserve Bank, dated April 23, 1914

We, the undersigned, hereby certify that this bank has an unimpaired capital of $50,000.

and surplus of $10,000 as shown by the books at the close of business on the 23rd

day of April, 1914.

(To be signed by three or more directors.)

R. N. Garrett — C. P. McKinney

Albert Rowell

R. K. Pinnyton

Directors.

NOTE.—If 6 per cent of the capital and surplus above shown amounts to a sum not divisible by 100, any excess or fractional part of $100 will entitle the applying bank to one additional share of stock. Accordingly in filling out the subscription on the reverse side of this form, the sum representing 6 per cent of the capital and surplus should be divided by 100 in order to obtain the number of shares to be applied for, and if an excess of less than $100 remains, one additional share should be added to the application, and included in the subscription of stock to be paid for at par in accordance with the provisions of the Federal Reserve Act.

LOCATION OF APPLYING BANK.

(Please fill in.)

City or Town El Dorado

County Union

State Arkansas

(Do not fill in below this line.)

Capital and surplus checked by

Entered in Register by

Number of shares verified by

Subscription entered in ledger by

Acknowledgment mailed by

Filed by

2—7458

Figure 15. Application for stock in the Federal Reserve Bank, page 2

Local Competition

Charles Murphy moved from Oakland, Louisiana to serve as the executor of J.F. Sample's estate. Among the assets of the estate was The Union County Bank in El Dorado. Sample had been one of the incorporators and president of the bank. Murphy took control and by July 1904 had the name changed to Citizens National as it was converted from a State to a National Bank.

The Citizens National and The First National grew and prospered. In September 1917, The Citizens had twice the dollar value of loans as The First National which had a greater number of deposits. Another competitor was established: The Exchange Bank, which was state chartered, and opened in 1924.

no. W. Hicks
DENTIST
t National Bank Build'g

Dr. Jno. W.
DENTIST
Office First National B

The El Dorado Times.

V. No. 3 —Established in 1894. EL DORADO, ARKANSAS, THURSDAY, SEPTEMBER 20, 1917. Subscription $1.5

....SAFETY AND SERVICE....

THE FIRST NATIONAL BANK

EL DORADO, ARKANSAS

STATEMENT OF FINANCIAL CONDITION AS MADE UNDER CALL OF COMPTROLLER OF THE CURRENCY AT WASHINGTON, D. C., SEPTEMBER, 11, 1917.

RESOURCES:	
Loans and Discounts	$156,502.74
U. S. Bonds to secure Circulation	12,510.00
U. S. Certificates of Indebtedness	25,000.00
U. S. Liberty Loan Bonds	47,446.70
Other Bonds and Securities	3,339.05
Stock in Federal Reserve Bank	1,800.00
Banking House, Furniture and Fixtures	22,000.00
Other Real Estate Owned	8,081.14
Redemption Fund	625.50
Cash and Due From Banks	140,840.10
Total	$418,145.23

LIABILITIES:	
Capital Stock	$50,000.00
Surplus and Profits	25,894.47
Circulation	12,210.00
Dividends Unpaid	60.00
DEPOSITS	329,980.76
Total	$418,145.23

"We want Your B[...]king Business"

DIREC[...]S:

R. N. Garrett C. P. McHenry R. K. P[...]er B. W. Reeves Albert Rowell

Figure 16. The First National Bank financial statement, dated September 11, 1917

WE STARTED

ith the RIGHT FOUNDATION in 190

We Have Been Growing and Are Still Growing

No. 7323

CONDENSED STATEMENT

OF THE CONDITION OF

he Citizens National Bank

OF EL DORADO, ARKANSAS

As made to the Comptroller of the Currency at the close of business, September 11th, 1917

RESOURCEES:

Loans and Discounts		$325,645.31
Overdrafts		NONE
Bonds and Securities		41,646.58
Banking House and Fixtures		4,501.00
Other Real Estate Owned		24.35
CASH:		
In Vault and Exchange	$120,655.64	
Loans on Cotton and Linters	46,179.59	
U. S. Liberty Bonds and Loans on Same	39,182.26	206,017.49
Total		$577,834.73

LIABILITIES:

Capital Stock, paid in	60,000.00
Surplus Fund	60,000.00
Undivided Profits	32,763.94
Circulation	32,500.00
Bills Payable	40,000.00
Deposits	285,184.61
Rediscounts, With Federal Reserve Banks	67,386.18
Total	$577,834.75

WE SOLICIT YOUR BANKING BUSINESS

ECTORS: H. C. McKINNEY H. L. BER M. W. HARDY W. J. MILES C. H. MURR

Figure 17. The Citizens National Bank financial statement, dated September 11, 1917

Restructure and Oil Boom

Internal changes were being made in The First National. M. Gordon Wade, son of Mattie Wade, was employed as a bookkeeper in October 1906. The later withdrawal of R.D. Duncan from the affairs of the bank and the subsequent sale of his stock created a shift in the balance of power.

R.N. Garrett supplanted B.W., Reeves as President of the Bank in 1909.

In 1919, B.W. Reeves resigned his position, as did Albert Rowell the cashier. They chartered a new state bank under Arkansas law and named it The Bank of Commerce. Albert Rowell was named president. They opened on October 1, 1919, and by 1923 had converted to a national charter to become the National Bank of Commerce.

A momentous event for the city of El Dorado happened on the afternoon of January 10, 1921. An oil well being drilled on the western edge of town blew in. A real gusher. Oil pushed up over the top of the rig and sprayed the area a mile around. Known as the Busey Well No. 1, it was the first successful oil well in Union County. Within days, this small town was overrun by people with intent to strike it rich.

Figure 18. The Busey Well #1, dated January 10, 1921

Figure 19. A team of mules pulls supplies through an oil field in El Dorado, Arkansas

Consolidation

Weeks after oil was struck in El Dorado, Charles Murphy left his office at Citizens Bank and walked the block on the south side of the Courthouse Square to the office of R.N. Garrett, president of The First National Bank. Murphy told Garrett that, in his opinion, to meet the demands of increased business, The Citizens and The First National should combine their resources and personnel to make one bank. Garrett agreed. After meetings with accountants, attorneys and regulators, a document entitled "Agreement of Consolidation Between The First National Bank of El Dorado (Ark) and The Citizens National Bank of El Dorado (Ark) Under the Titles of The First National Bank of El Dorado" was executed on March 26, 1921.

A letter of approval from the Comptroller of The Currency of the Treasury Department in Washington was dated June 4, 1921.

The Board of Directors of the bank after consolidation were: R.N. Garrett, C.P McHenry, J.A. Rowland, W.F. McWilliams, H. Wade, M.G. Wade, H.C. McKinney, C.H. Murphy, W.J. Miles, M.W. Hardy, and H.C. Berg.

Officers:

Chairman of the Board	R.N. Garrett
President	H.C. McKinney
Vice President	C.H. Murphy
Cashier	M.G. Wade
Assistant Cashiers	F.W. Miles
	L. Wilson
	H.W. Cawthon
	J.A. Blakely
	D.M. Yocum
	F.E. Roney

After the merger of The Citizens and The First National Bank, the building on the southwest corner of Main and Washington streets was vacated. All personnel and banking services were moved to the building at the southwest corner of Main at Jefferson streets.

TREASURY DEPARTMENT

OFFICE OF THE

COMPTROLLER OF THE CURRENCY.

Washington, D. C., June 4, 1921.

Whereas, by satisfactory evidence presented to the undersigned, it has been made to appear that the directors and shareholders of The First National Bank of El Dorado, Arkansas, and The Citizens National Bank of El Dorado, Arkansas, have complied with all the provisions of an Act of Congress approved November 7, 1918, entitled "An Act to provide for the consolidation of National Banking Associations":

Now, therefore, I, D. R. Crissinger, Comptroller of the Currency, do hereby certify that The First National Bank of El Dorado, and The Citizens National Bank of El Dorado have been consolidated under the charter and corporate title of "The First National Bank of El Dorado", with Capital Stock of Three Hundred and Fifty Thousand Dollars ($350,000) and that the said consolidation is approved.

In testimony whereof witness my hand and seal of office this Fourth day of June, 1921.

D R Crissinger
Comptroller of the Currency.

Charter No. 7046 Consolidation No. 51.

Figure 20. Comptroller approval of the consolidation of The First National Bank and Citizens National Bank

Wh Ao

OFFICE OF
COMPTROLLER OF THE CURRENCY
ADDRESS REPLY TO
COMPTROLLER OF THE CURRENCY

TREASURY DEPARTMENT

WASHINGTON

June 4, 1921.

Cashier,
The First National Bank,
El Dorado, Arkansas.

Sir:

There is inclosed certificate issued today approving the consolidation of your association and The Citizens National Bank of El Dorado, under the provisions of the Act of November 7, 1918, under the charter and corporate title of "The First National Bank of El Dorado." You have been advised by telegraph of the approval.

Please advise whether The Citizens National Bank of El Dorado is a depositary for postal savings funds. This information is desired as it will be necessary to give the Post Office Department authorization to make the necessary transfer of funds in connection with the consolidation.

Please also send to this office at your earliest convenience a certified list of shareholders of the consolidated bank, giving the names, residences and number of shares owned by each shareholder, together with a statement of condition of the consolidated bank as shown by its books at close of business on the date of consolidation, June 4, 1921. You should also furnish this office with the oaths of directors and signatures of the officers of the consolidated bank. Blanks are inclosed. Data called for on the back of the blank form of condition is not required.

Respectfully,

Deputy Comptroller.

Inc.

6-14-21
Sent Statement
List of Directors
Report of appointment and signatures of officers
Certified list of Shareholders.
Joint oath of directors
oath of Director Henry L Berg.

Figure 21. Consolidation approval letter from the U.S. Treasury Department

2

AGREEMENT OF CONSOLIDATION

between

The FIRST NATIONAL BANK OF EL DORADO,

and

The CITIZENS NATIONAL BANK OF EL DORADO,

under the title of

The FIRST NATIONAL BANK OF EL DORADO,

---+---

THIS AGREEMENT made between The FIRST NATIONAL BANK OF EL DORADO, and The CITIZENS NATIONAL BANK OF EL DORADO, , each located in EL DORADO, ARKANSAS, , and each acting pursuant to a resolution of its Board of Directors and by a majority of said Boards, pursuant to the authority given by, and in accordance with the provisions of, an Act of the Congress of the United States entitled "An Act to provide for the consolidation of national banking associations", approved on the 7th day of November, 1918, witnesseth as follows:

1. The FIRST NATIONAL BANK OF EL DORADO (hereafter referred to as the FIRST PARTY,) and The CITIZENS NATIONAL BANK OF EL DORADO (hereafter referred to as the SECOND PARTY) are hereby consolidated under the charter of the said first-named association as hereby modified.

2. The name of the consolidated association shall be " THE FIRST NATIONAL BANK OF EL DORADO ".

3. The amount of capital stock of the consolidated association shall be THREE HUNDRED FIFTY THOUSAND & NO/100 dollars ($350.000), divided into THIRTY-FIVE HUNDRED shares (3,500.00) of one hundred dollars ($100.00) each, subject to the right to change the amount of said capital hereafter as

Figure 22. Consolidation agreement details within approval letter, page 2

is now or shall hereafter be authorized by law. On the date of consolidation its surplus shall be TWENTY-FOUR THOUSAND dollars ($ 24,000.00). Said capital, surplus and undivided profits at the date of consolidation shall then aggregate THREE HUNDRED SEVENTY-FOUR THOUSAND, dollars ($374,000.00). Of this capital SEVENTEEN HUNDRED FIFTY, (1,750.00) shares shall be allotted to the present shareholders of The FIRST NATIONAL BANK OF EL DORADO being THREE AND ONE-HALF shares for each share now held by them, and SEVENTEEN-HUNDRED FIFTY (1,750) shall be allotted to the present shareholders of The CITIZENS NATIONAL BANK OF EL DORADO being TWO AND ELEVEN-TWELFTHS for each share now held by them. The assets contributed by each of said associations shall, upon the effective date of the consolidation, be passed upon and be acceptable to a committee of six, three to be appointed by the Board of Directors of each association, and the shareholders of the present FIRST -PARTY shall furnish net assets above all liabilities of that association equal to ONE HUNDRED EIGHTY-SEVEN THOUSAND DOLLARS of the capital and surplus and undivided profits of the consolidated bank, and the present shareholders of The SECOND PARTY, shall furnish net assets equal to ONE HUNDRED EIGHTY-SEVEN THOUSAND DOLLARS. Such assets of either association as it shall not consider desirable to carry into the consolidation, or as shall not be necessary to make up its contribution to the capital, surplus and undivided profits, as aforesaid, shall be transferred by it, before the effective date of the consolidation, to a Trustee or Trustees for the ultimate benefit of its shareholders, upon whatever terms and under whatever conditions shall be deemed proper. In the event that there is not sufficient net assets in either association to make good its proportion of capital and surplus and undivided profits of ($374,000.00) herein

Figure 23. Consolidation agreement details, page 3

4

provided for, the shareholders of the association not having sufficient assets to make good its proportion shall pay the difference in cash.

The Board of Directors of the consolidated bank shall consist of not fewer than FIVE nor more than FIFTEEN shareholders, and the following named directors shall constitute the Board for the remainder of the year:

R. N. GARRETT,
M. G. WADE,
C. P. McHENRY,
J. A. ROWLAND,
W. F. McWILLIAMS,
HOPKINS WADE,
H. C. McKINNEY.
C. H. MURPHY.
W. J. MILES.
M. W. HARDY.
H. L. BERG,

Figure 24. Consolidation agreement details, page 4

4. This consolidation shall become effective when it shall have been ratified and confirmed by the affirmative vote of the shareholders of each of said associations owning at least two-thirds of its capital stock outstanding, at a meeting to be held pursuant to a call dy the Directors heretofore made, and shall have been approved by the Comptroller of the Currency of the United States.

WITNESS the signatures and seals of said associations, this 8TH day of APRIL 1921 each hereunto set by the President and attested by its Cashier, pursuant to a resolution of its Board of Directors, acting by a majority thereof, and witness the signatures hereto of a majority of each of said Boards of Directors.

The FIRST NATIONAL BANK OF EL DORADO,

by R. N. GARRETT, President.

ATTEST:

M. G. WADE, Cashier.

(SEAL).

R. N. GARRETT.
M. G. WADE.
C. P. McHENRY.
J. A. ROWLAND.
HOPKINS WADE.

Directors of the FIRST National Bank of ELDORADO,

Figure 25. Consolidation agreement details, page 5

6

The CITIZENS NATIONAL BANK OF EL DORADO,

by H. C. McKINNEY,
President.

ATTEST:

C. H. MURPHY,
Cashier.

(SEAL)

H. C. McKINNEY.

C. H. MURPHY.

M. W. HARDY.

W. J. MILES.

Directors of the CITIZENS National Bank of EL DORADO

STATE OF ARKANSAS)
)ss.
COUNTY OF UNION)

On this 8TH day of APRIL, , 1921 before me, a Notary Public for the State and County aforesaid, personally came R. N. GARRETT, , as President, and M. G. WADE, , as Cashier of The FIRST National Bank of EL DORADO , and each in his said capacity acknowledged the foregoing instrument to be the act and deed of said association and the seal affixed thereto to be its seal; and came also

R. N. GARRETT , M. G. WADE , J. A. ROWLAND. ,
C. P. McHENRY, HOPKINS WADE, , , ,
, , ,

Figure 26. Consolidation agreement details, page 6

7

being a majority of the Board of Directors of said association, and each of them acknowledged said instrument to be the act and deed of said association and of himself as a director thereof.

WITNESS my official seal and signature this day and year aforesaid.

My commission expires JANY. 25, 1925.

(SEAL).

W. J. PINSON,
Notary Public, UNION County.

STATE OF ARKANSAS,)
)ss:
COUNTY OF UNION)

On this 8TH day of APRIL, 1921, before me, a Notary Public for the State and County aforesaid, personally came H. C. MCKINNEY, as President, and C. H. MURPHY, as Cashier of The CITIZENS National Bank of EL DORADO, and each in his said capacity acknowledged the foregoing instrument to be the act and deed of said association and the seal affixed thereto to be its seal; and came also

H. C. MCKINNEY, C. H. MURPHY, H. W. HARDY.
W. J. MILES,

being a majority of the Board of Directors of said association, and each of them acknowledged said instrument to be the act and deed of said association and of himself as a director thereof.

WITNESS my official seal and signature this day and year aforesaid.

My commission expires JANY. 25, 1925.

(S E A L)

W. J. PINSON,
Notary Public, UNION County.

Figure 27. Consolidation agreement details, page 7

Building History

The 1902 construction of a brick building on the southwest corner of Main and Washington streets initiated a series of events that proved tragic for the owners, the Parnell family. A dispute over the sidewalk access between the Parnell's and the town Marshal, Guy Tucker, added to existing grievances between them. This longstanding feud led to a gunfight on the courthouse square on October 9, 1902, with the Marshal Tucker wounded and Tom and Walter Parnell dead. On November 3, 1902, the title to the corner property was deeded from A.L. Parnell to J.M. Parnell. A lease agreement was executed on March 23, 1903 between Swilley, Sorrells, and Co. and J.M. Parnell on said property for 5 years. Terms included monthly lease payments and the right of purchase at a stipulated price during the lease term. On October 5, 1903, Swilley, Sorrells, and Co. leased part of the property to B.W. Reeves to use as a bank building. Several months later, the bank signed an agreement with W.M. Swilley on March 25, 1904 to purchase the entirety of the property for the bank. The bank's growth necessitated the construction of a larger building in 1910. This building was used with renovations until 1921.

The vacated building was torn down and a new bank building that still stands today was erected. A grand opening of this new building was held on April 11, 1922.

No 7046

The First National Bank

B. W. REEVES, PRESIDENT
R. N. GARRETT, FIRST VICE-PRESIDENT
C. P. McHENRY, SECOND VICE-PRESIDENT
ALBERT ROWELL, CASHIER

EL DORADO, ARK.,

MEMORANDA OF AGREEMENT WITH

W. M. Swilley & Bro.

In the matter of the lot and building occupied by the First National Bank of El Dorado, it was agreed between the said Swilley & Bro and R. D. Duncan representing the First National Bank, that said Swilley & Bro. should purchase from Parnell, the owner of the property now occupied by Swilley & Bro. and the First National Bank, for ~~$5882.00~~ 6250, the optional price named in the lease of said property to Swilley Sorrells & Co: and that said Swilley & Bro should sell to said First National Bank 27 1/2 feet, more or less, by 70 feet more or less, and the part of building that covers said ground, for ~~$2941.00~~ 3125.

It was further underst od and agreed that the said First National Bank should loan to the said Swilley & Bro ~~$2941.00~~ 3125 for twelve months at 10%, with which to pay for their half of the above mentioned property, said loan to be securred by deed of trust on that part of the propergy retained by said Swilley & Bro.

Albert Rowell Cashier
R. D. Duncan
W. M. Swilley & Bro

El Dorado, Arkansas.

March 25th, 1904.

July 17, 1905 renewed

Figure 28. Property purchase agreement, dated March 25, 1904 and renewed on July 17, 1905

FIRST NATIONAL BANK *In the fall of 1903, a group of local businessmen organized The First National Bank of El Dorado, listing capital of $25,000.00. The bank opened for business on December 9 of that year in a small, one-story brick building on the southwest corner of Main and Washington streets. In 1921, First National consolidated with Citizens National Bank and opened its doors to the public the following year in a new, three-story structure. Although many renovations, expansions and branch locations have been added, the bank still serves its customers from that main location downtown.*

Figure 29. Illustration of property purchased March 25, 1904

Figure 30. The First National Bank building

Figure 31. The Citizens National Bank building in 1921

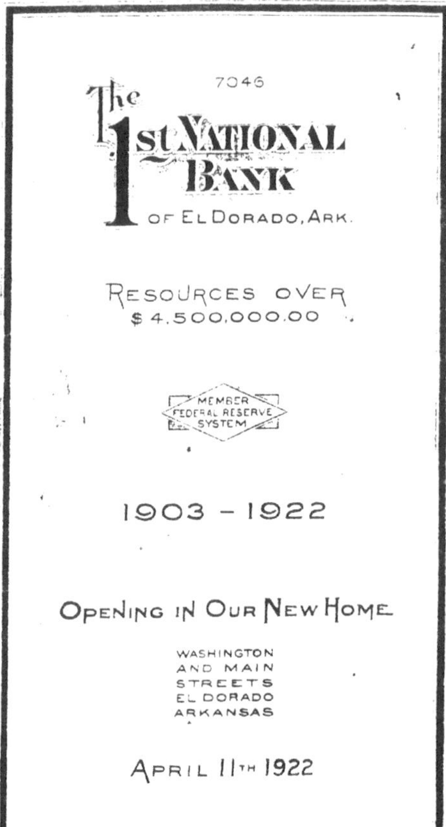

INFORMATION FOR GUESTS

In order to avoid confusion and insure that everyone will be given an opportunity to view our new banking quarters in an orderly manner, we have arranged that the guests will be carried through the building in charge of ushers.

Upon entering the building this booklet is to be handed the guests, and they will then be directed to a registry desk, where their name, address and business will be recorded in a registry book and they will be handed a card upon which will appear two numbers corresponding to the registry number. In the route through the building they will pass by a window where a souvenir will be exchanged for one of these numbers. At another window the other number will be deposited in a ballot box from which at the close of the reception a number will be drawn, which will designate the recipients of two prizes to be awarded.

Children will not be registered and will, therefore, not participate in the prizes.

We assure you that you are a welcome guest and we trust that our new home will be a source of enjoyment and benefit to you.

Figure 32. Grand opening brochure of newly merged *First National Bank of El Dorado, Ark.*

THE FIRST NATIONAL BANK OF EL DORADO

1903-1922

The First National Bank of El Dorado was organized and opened for business in December, 1903, occupying a one-story brick building on the southwest corner of Main Street and Washington Avenue. At that time the population of El Dorado was probably not more than one thousand people, and the First National Bank was one of the few National Banks in the State of Arkansas.

The original capital of the First National Bank was $25,000.00, which is the smallest capital permitted under the National Banking Act. With a substantial growth of El Dorado and a constant increase of business the capital stock was increased several years after the organization to $50,000.00, and a much larger and more modern banking house was erected in 1910. This building served the Bank well for several years, until the discovery of the El Dorado field and the bringing in of the famous Busey well January 10, 1921, at which time the building became entirely inadequate for the great increase of business.

The Citizens National Bank was organized in July, 1904, about seven months after the organization of First National, with paid in capital of $50,000.00, operating at the corner of Main and Jefferson. In 1907 the capital stock was increased to $60,000.00, at which figure it remained as long as they did business under the name of Citizens National Bank.

After the discovery of oil in our community and the realization that the condition was not merely a boom, but of a permanent nature, the officers of First National Bank and Citizens National Bank saw the very pressing need for a larger and stronger institution at El Dorado and conceived the idea of effecting a consolidation of the two banks.

This consolidation was agreed upon by the Boards of Directors of the banks mentioned and after the requirements of the Treasury Department had been met the Comptroller of the Currency approved the merger which became effective June 6, 1921.

The consolidated banks, or the Greater First National Bank, opened for business on Monday, June 6th, 1921, with a capital of $350,000.00 and Surplus and Profits of $77,500.00, the following being Directors as provided in the consolidation agreement:

R. N. GARRETT	H. C. McKINNEY
C. P. McHENRY	C. H. MURPHY
J. A. ROWLAND	W. J. MILES
W. F. McWILLIAMS	M. W. HARDY
H. WADE	H. L. BERG

M. G. WADE

At the first meeting of the Board of Directors of the consolidated bank, the following Officers were elected:

R. N. GARRETT, Chairman of the Board
H. C. McKINNEY, President
C. H. MURPHY, Vice-President
M. G. WADE, Cashier
F. W. MILES, Assistant Cashier
L. WILSON, Assistant Cashier
H. W. CAWTHON, Assistant Cashier

Figure 33. Grand opening brochure of newly merged *First National Bank of El Dorado, Ark.*, pages 2-3

I. A. BLAKELY, Assistant Cashier
D. M. YOCUM, Assistant Cashier
F. E. RONEY, Assistant Cashier

It is with pardonable pride we trust that we refer to the personnel of the above Directors and Officers; all citizens of our community who have lived here and are men of unquestioned standing and character, tried and not found wanting.

DESCRIPTION OF THE NEW BUILDING AND EQUIPMENT

The new home of the First National Bank has been erected on a lot forty-six by ninety feet and is constructed of reinforced concrete and steel; it is as near fire-proof as a building can be made, very little wood of any kind having been used in the finished building.

The fixtures in the Banking Room are of the Tennessee marble and bronze and are of the most modern design. The Paying and Receiving windows, the Savings Department window and Exchange windows are on the west side of the central lobby. The Statement window and the Collection and Escrow windows are on the south side of the lobby. The Loan Department and officers' desks are on the east side of the lobby. The main cash vault is located in the south end of the building and is of latest construction throughout. The walls of this vault, as well as those of the Safe Deposit vault in the basement, are of the most modern approved construction from the standpoint of strength and security, being constructed of poured concrete twenty inches thick, reinforced by steel rods of tensile strength of 30,000 pounds to the inch, running horizontally and vertically. The openings of these vaults are protected by massive steel doors as well as time locks which offer absolute protection to the funds and valuables of this bank and its customers.

We wish to call special attention to our Safe Deposit Department. This department is located in the basement of the building and is entered by a wide stairway which leads from the main lobby to the basement. We have had installed Safe Deposit boxes, large and small, in ample number to supply the present need of our customers and we have room in the vault to add to these boxes as the demand increases. Each box is of the latest and best construction, being equipped with guard locks as well as locks with keys for the customer.

There is nothing so disturbing to the peace of one's mind as the fear of misplacing or losing important papers, jewelry, or other valuables. We consider the vaults of the First National Bank as strong as it is possible to make them, and your bonds and other valuables when in our vaults will be securely protected against burglary, theft and fire.

We have unbounded faith in the future of our oil field, our City and our State. We believe our home and equipment is as new and complete as can be found, and we take pride in dedicating our new home to the future greatness of a Greater El Dorado.

Figure 34. Grand opening brochure of newly merged *First National Bank of El Dorado, Ark.*, pages 4-5

EMPLOYEES

J. B. LASSITER, Auditor
MISS LILLIE WILSON, Discount Teller
MISS HELEN McRAE, Discount Teller
H. W. CAWTHON, Transit Teller
E. F. SPAWR, Escrow Teller
MISS MARY NORRIS, Paying and Receiving Teller
H. B. GRACE, Paying and Receiving Teller
E. R. CHIDESTER, Paying and Receiving Teller
JOHN LIPPS, Paying and Receiving Teller
RALPH A. REYNOLDS, Paying and Receiving Teller
E. N. EWING, Paying and Receiving Teller
MISS LEILA HARMAN, Savings Teller
W. S. SLOAN, Exchange Teller
SAM W. JOSLYN, Collection Teller
MISS ANN CORDELL, Rental Clerk
F. W. MILES, General Bookkeeper
J. H. SHORT, Head Bookkeeper
P. F. KNOTTS, Individual Bookkeeper
E. E. BLEVINS, Individual Bookkeeper
J. H. BUCKLEY, Individual Bookkeeper
A. B. COLLINS, Individual Bookkeeper
CARL B. FARMER, Individual Bookkeeper
JAMES R. FULLER, Individual Bookkeeper
MISS ETHEL KEYS, Statement Department
MURPHY SANDLIN, Statement Department
MISS RUBY DUCOTE, Transit Department
MISS LAURA DUCOTE, Transit Department
W. E. GOODWIN, Pivot Clerk
C. F. CARGILE, Pivot Clerk
MISS KATHRYN McRAE, Stenographer
ZELL SMITH, Information and New Accounts
MISS RUTH ALICE WILSON, Safe Deposit Department
WATT SMITH, Runner

CONDENSED STATEMENT OF THE CONDITION OF

THE FIRST NATIONAL BANK

EL DORADO, ARKANSAS
No. 7046

As Made to the Comptroller of Currency at the Close of Business
March 10th, 1922

RESOURCES

Loans and Discounts	$2,377,760.43
Bankers' Acceptances	501,134.14
U. S. Liberty Bonds and Certificates of Indebtedness	262,891.58
Stock in Federal Reserve Bank	11,250.00
U. S. Bonds to Secure Circulation	45,010.00
Bonds, Securities, Etc.	109,724.10
Banking House, Furniture and Fixtures	102,879.45
Other Real Estate Owned	7,829.52
Interest Earned, Not Collected	187.37
Other Assets	564.58
Cash in Vault, Exchange, and U. S. Treasury	1,142,044.34
Total	$4,561,275.51

LIABILITIES

Capital Stock	$ 350,000.00
Surplus and Profits	122,965.34
Discount Collected, Not Earned	25,837.51
Circulation	45,010.00
DEPOSITS	4,017,462.66
Total	$4,561,275.51

Figure 35. Grand opening brochure of newly merged *First National Bank of El Dorado, Ark.*, pages 6-7

OFFICERS:

R.N. GARRETT	CHAIRMAN OF THE BOARD
H. C. McKINNEY	PRESIDENT
C.H. MURPHY	VICE PRESIDENT
F. E. RONEY	VICE PRESIDENT
M. G. WADE	CASHIER
F. W. MILES	ASS'T CASHIER
L. WILSON	ASS'T CASHIER
H. W. CAWTHON	ASS'T CASHIER
W. S. SLOAN	ASS'T CASHIER

DIRECTORS:

R. N. GARRETT

H. C. McKINNEY

C. H. MURPHY

F. E. RONEY

M. G. WADE

J. A. ROWLAND

W. J. MILES

C. P. McHENRY

M. W. HARDY

HOPKINS WADE

W. F. McWILLIAMS

Figure 36. Grand opening brochure of newly merged *First National Bank of El Dorado, Ark.*, page 8

Through the Years

The bank and its competitors survived the Great Depression, World War II, as well as the slowdown in oil production.

In 1953, The First National Bank celebrated its 50th Anniversary.

Through the mid-1950s, the bank building underwent major updates with exterior and interior renovations. An additional section was built on the west side of the building.

Drive-through banking was introduced to El Dorado in 1960. The facility, located at the southeast corner of Washington and Cedar streets, was physically attached to the main bank building by underground tubes. Cylindrical containers carried money and documents between the bank and the drive-in. Three more branch facilities were built as banking laws and regulations were relaxed in the 1960s and 70s.

In 1965, the board of directors began discussing the potential need for expanding the bank's properties. The first conversations continued around the merits of purchasing the remainder of the north half of the block as it fronted on Main Street. When efforts to obtain the properties were stalled, the focus shifted towards acquiring the south half of the block. This was the site of the Garrett Hotel and its parking lot. The bank bought the buildings and the entire parcel of land in November 1968. The hotel closed down, the contents were sold, and the building was razed.

Figure 37. New Drive-through banking location, established in 1960

Figure 38. Drive-through banking North location, established in the mid 1960s

Figure 39. *The First National Bank* lobby, 1956

Figure 40. *The First National Bank* building, 1950s

Figure 41. Facade of *The First National Bank* building, 1950s

Figure 42. Pictured left to right: W.D. (Bill) Meacham, Ann Cordell, H.C. (Henry) McKinney Jr.

Construction

A contract was signed with the Austin Company of Houston, Texas to design and construct the banking offices on the Garrett site. The design as approved was to construct a three-story building. The first level would be underground, the second level would incorporate the south entrance and open on to Cedar Street, and the third level would serve as the main banking area and be at the same elevation as the existing bank lobby.

The structure was designed to accommodate the addition of two more floors as needed for future expansion. The walls and partitions that defined the banking lobby of the older building were removed to create a converted plaza entrance to the new bank building. Construction was completed and the building was occupied by bank personnel in the Fall of 1974.

Figure 43. Illustration of *The First National Bank* building, 1974

Figure 44. *The First National Bank* building, 1980s

New Wave

A change in management in 1973 was the prelude to a new era of bank consolidations. That year, Gordon Parker moved from California to El Dorado to be president of The First National. He brought with him a cultural experience of small banks being sold to large banks by way of a holding company.

Articles of Incorporation for First United Bancshares, Inc. were filed August 8, 1980 with the State of Arkansas. The incorporators were Gordon E. Parker, C.H. Murphy Jr., and H.C. McKinney, Jr.

In December 1, 1980 an association under the title of First National Bank of El Dorado was created under the provisions of United State Code. In addition to the three incorporators of the holding company (Parker, Murphy, and McKinney), the following shareholders were also listed: Michael F. Mahony, Richard H. Mason and Dr.

David M. Yocum, Jr.

December 18, 1980 the shareholders of First National Bank met and agreed to a merger with The First National after the stock of The First National Bank was exchanged for the stock of First United Bancshares, Inc.

December 30, 1980 the shareholders of the First National Bank of El Dorado agree to a Plan of Reorganization to exchange their shares of Bank Common Stock on a share-for-share basis for Common Stock of First United Bancshares, Inc.

With the plan approved by federal regulators in the Spring of 1981, the "interim" bank First National was merged into The First National Bank.

First United Bancshares continued to be successful in acquiring Banks in Arkansas, Texas, and Louisiana over a span approaching 20 years.

Figure 45. Bank executives in the late 1970s. Pictured left to right: Robert Dudley Sr. (Executive VP), H.C. McKinney, Jr. (Chairman), Arlen Waldrup (VP and Trust Officer), Gordon Parker (President), James Y. Cameron (VP)

Final Phase and Key People

In the year 2000, First United Bancshares, Inc. entered negotiations to become a part of Bancorpsouth of Tupelo, Mississippi. By September, the sale of First United and its affiliate banks was completed. The First National Bank of El Dorado as a corporate entity ceased to exist.

R.D. DUNCAN was born in Claysville, Kentucky in 1858, and moved with his parents and siblings to St. Joseph, Missouri in 1870. He graduated from William Jewell College in Liberty, Missouri. In May 1885, he married Adelaide J. Corbin of Liberty. Two sons were born of this marriage, both of whom were deceased in the 1950s, one in Arkansas and the other in Pennsylvania. Adelaide died and was buried in Liberty in 1908.

R.D. Duncan started his career with the Central Savings Bank of St. Joseph,

Missouri. He resigned as the cashier of the Central Savings Bank as of January 1, 1896, at which time he moved to Kansas City to work in the live-stock commissions business. He and his family were in Kansas City in 1900 as recorded by the U.S. Census that year. Duncan came to El Dorado in 1903. His credentials identity him as the assistant cashier of First National Bank of Paragould, Arkansas and resident of the same. In conversations with bank officials and the Greene County Historical Society, we find no evidence of his presence there. Duncan changed his address in our bank records in December 1903 from Paragould, Arkansas to St. Louis, Missouri. According to court documents, the State National Bank of Little Rock, Arkansas was organized in 1902, naming William H. Garanflo as president and Robert D. Duncan as vice president and cashier. In 1908 an advertisement in the Arkansas Gazette for the sale of stock of the Ozark Diamond Mining Company lists R.D. Duncan as one of the directors. He identifies himself as Auditor of the Bankers' Trust Company of St. Louis, Mo.

In June of 1914, the State National Bank of Little Rock closed its doors and went through liquidation. Garanflo and Duncan were both indicted on five counts of willful misapplication of the money, funds, and credits of the State National Bank, and a sixth count of conspiring to misapply the money, funds, and credits of the State National Bank. A jury trial in April 1916 found them guilty on all counts. An appeal in November 1917 resulted in the convictions being upheld. Both defendants, Garanflo and Duncan, were sentenced to six years in a federal penitentiary in Atlanta, Georgia.

Duncan was incarcerated in July 1918. He was released in May 1920, after serving less than two years of the six-year sentence. A pardon was granted to him by the President of the United States, Woodrow Wilson. William H. Garanflo was pardoned and released two weeks before Duncan. My opinion is that two factors influenced the decision to pardon them. First, there was a campaign of businesspeople in Little Rock that petitioned for Garanflo's release. The other is that the liquidation of the State National Bank resulted in the depositors being paid. R.D. Duncan was nearing 62 years of age at the time of his release from prison. I have no additional information on his activities. One source suggests he died in Missouri in the mid-1930s.

MATTIE C.R. WADE was born October 9, 1861. Her maiden name was Mattie Carolyn Ramsey. She married Hopkins Wade and their union resulted in four children: Maxwell Gordon Wade, Maud Wade, Nellie Wade, and Hopkins Wade, Jr. Her husband died in 1893. She moved to El Dorado in 1894. Her late husband had operated a general store in Blanchard Springs in the southern part of Union County. In El Dorado she became associated with the El Dorado Dry Goods Company which was incorporated in 1899 by C.P. McHenry, W.J. Bryant, and W.J. Miles. McHenry was one of the first subscribers for stock in the proposed National Bank of El Dorado, and this may be one of the reasons Mattie Wade became a subscriber. It should be noted that the initial subscription listing shows Mattie Wade with 20 shares, which is second in number to only R.D. Duncan who took 120 shares for his efforts. The next highest to Mattie was 15 shares, and the rest were in the range of 1 to 10 shares. These numbers changed a few times before the Bank was approved and became operational. As noted earlier, her election to the board in December 1903 was unusual as women had not yet been extended political voting rights. Surely this was a testament to her abilities as a businesswoman. She continued her relationship with the bank through her sons. Mattie Wade was 92 years of age when she died December 15th, 1953.

Figure 46. M. Gordon Wade

M. GORDON WADE, elder son of Mattie Wade, started his career with The First National Bank in October 1906. He advanced to the position of assistant cashier in March of 1908. He was named cashier in July 1919 and was elected to the board of directors in September 1919. Gordon Wade was elected president of the bank in 1942 and remained so until retirement on December 31, 1950. Wade knew tragedy in his personal life. His first wife died in 1911. A son was born in 1911 and died in 1922. In 1924, Gordon Wade married Blanche Parnell, whose father was killed in the 1902 Parnell-Tucker feud shoot out. Gordon Wade died in 1971. Blanche Wade died in El Dorado in 1995 at age 97.

HOPKINS WADE was the son of Mattie Wade and younger brother of M. Gordon. Wade was a director on the bank board in the 1920s and 1930s. He died in 1939.

B.W. REEVES migrated from Georgia to South Arkansas after the Civil War. With financial help from W.D. Gresham, he bought land and built a general store in downtown El Dorado in 1879. Reeves called a meeting in his office which resulted in the formation of the Bank of El Dorado, of which he became president. This bank failed. R.D. Duncan came to El Dorado to organize a bank and Reeves became involved and was named the first president. In 1919 he ended his relationship with The First National Bank to be a founder of the Bank of Commerce. His mercantile business continued to prosper into the mid-60s.

R.N. GARRETT was one of the organizers of The First National Bank. He was elected as a director and first-vice president of the bank. A few years later he became president, with B.W. Reeves being named first-vice president. With the consolidation of the banks in 1921, he became chairman of the board of directors and continued in that office until his death in 1942. He built the Garrett Hotel in 1912 and was involved in a number of other successful local businesses.

Figure 47. R.N. Garrett

H.C. MCKINNEY, SR. was a native of Union County. In 1899 he entered into a partnership with J.F. Sample to operate a mercantile business. The J.F Sample Company was incorporated in 1907 with McKinney as president, in which capacity he served for the rest of his life. He was a member of the board of directors of the Citizens National Bank. He was an inactive officer who held the title of president of the bank. He was named president of the combined banks after their consolidation in 1921, at which time he devoted his time to the bank. In 1942 he was elected chairman of the board, an office he held until his death in 1952.

Figure 48. H.C. McKinney, Sr.

H.C. MCKINNEY, JR. became an officer of the bank in 1935 and was elected to the board in 1937. Following the retirement of M. Gordon Wade, McKinney Jr. was named president of the bank in January 1951. He served in that capacity until July 1973 when he was elected chairman of the board of the bank. McKinney, Jr. died in January 1981.

Figure 49. H.C. McKinney, Jr.

C.H. MURPHY, SR. came to El Dorado in September 1904 to manage the assets of J.F. Sample's estate. He was elected president and member of the board of the Citizens National Bank. In 1906 he gave up his title as president and took the position of cashier and executive officer

Figure 50. Charles H. Murphy, Sr.

of the bank. This was a pattern of things to come. After successfully engineering the consolidation and construction, he was elected vice-president and executive officer of The First National Bank. He was consulted and made decisions on major issues related to the bank. Charles Murphy Sr. had wide and varied interests beyond banking. He was involved in overseeing farmlands, timberlands, and managing the exploration and production of oil and gas properties. He retired from active status as an officer of the bank in 1946 but retained a seat on the bank board until his death.

CHARLES H. MURPHY, JR. followed in the footsteps of his father and became a successful businessman at an early age. He returned from World War II with a vision of starting his own integrated oil company. Using the assets of the Murphy family interests he was able to create the Murphy Oil Corporation. The success of the company has been well documented. In the late 1960s he turned his attention to The First National Bank. He bought a considerable number of shares of bank stock. Charles initiated policies for the retirement of executive officers and directors. He was also involved in and was one of the three incorporators of the First United Bancshares, Inc.

Figure 51. Charles H. Murphy, Jr.

ALBERT ROWELL was a native of Missouri. He attended William Jewell College in Liberty, Missouri and lived and worked in Kearney which was near Liberty, Kansas City, and St. Josephs. I believe that he was known to R.D. Duncan. He was employed when the bank was formed in 1903 as the secretary and cashier. He would have been the first full-time employee with banking experience. He served as cashier until he resigned to become president of the newly founded Bank of Commerce in El Dorado.

Figure 52. Bank executives in the 1970s. Pictured (left to right): H.C. (Henry) McKinney, Jr., Gordon Parker, W.D. (Bill) Meacham

BANK DATA

1905

Copied from First Annual Calendar Public High School Library El Dorado, Ark.

No. 7046. *Josephine Rowell Hanna 5-21-1982*

THE FIRST NATIONAL BANK.

OFFICERS.

B. W. Reeves, *President* R. N. Garrett, *First Vice President*
C. P. McHenry, *Second Vice President* Albert Rowell, *Cashier*

Capital Stock, $25.000

BOARD OF DIRECTORS.

B. W. Reeves R. N. Garrett C. P. McHenry
Mrs. M. C. Wade R. D. Duncan

HISTORY OF THE FIRST NATIONAL BANK.

The First National Bank, of El Dorado was opened for business December 9, 1903. Its number in the list of all national banks to be established in the United States is 7046.

It was the first national bank to be organized in Union County; it was the sixteenth national bank in the State of Arkansas when established. Since the first charter issued to national banks in 1863 there have been 7,417 organized, of which number 5,457 with aggregate capital of $777,741,335, were in operation September 30, 1904. The average amount paid to the creditors of insolvent national banks is 78% on their claims. No national bank has ever failed where the officers and directors have observed the requirements of the national bank laws.

No. 7323.

CITIZENS NATIONAL BANK.

OFFICERS.

C. H. Murphy, *President* W. W. Brown, *Vice President*
M. W. Hardy, *Cashier* W. J. Pinson, *Second Vice President*
E. H. Hearin, *Assistant Cashier*

BOARD OF DIRECTORS.

W. J. Pinson W. W. Brown J. R. Miears W. M. Green
C. H. Murphy John C. Ritchie A. A. Tufts Henry L. Berg
Henry W. Myar

BENEFITS OF BANKS IN GENERAL.

1. When wisely and carefully managed they net the stockholder satisfactory return for his capital invested.
2. They gather the idle funds from the many secret hiding places and turn them again into useful channels of commerce.
3. They furnish the best mechanical safeguards, re-enforced by protective insurance against loss of funds by fire, and burglary.
4. They relieve the holder of cash assets of personal danger that always

Figure 53. History and 1905 Officers / Board Members of The First National Bank of El Dorado

1980s

First National Bank

1950s

1920s

1900s

THE NATIONAL BANK OF EL DORADO.

Influencers

Three generations of the Mahony family: J.K. Mahony, Emon A. Mahony, and Michael F. Mahony; two generations of the Nolan family: William C. Nolan and Robert C. Nolan; as well as H.S. Yocum Sr.; Dr. David M. Yocum Jr.; O.C. Bailey; J.D. Trimble; and Russell Marks all served as directors of the bank. They also served as members or chairman of sub-committees of the board on matters from executive compensation, employee benefits, health and pension plans, audit and federal law compliance, to lending practices and loan approvals.

I end this by saying thanks to H.C. McKinney, Jr. and W.D. Meacham. They took a chance to give me the opportunity to be a member of the First National family. Their integrity, honesty, and loyalty has made a lasting impression on my life.

www.ingramcontent.com/pod-product-compliance
Ingram Content Group UK Ltd.
Pitfield, Milton Keynes, MK11 3LW, UK
UKHW060106300726
14090UKWH00003B/384

* 9 7 9 8 2 1 8 1 0 0 4 8 3 *